What

What is Revival?

by
REV. G. J. MORGAN
Minister: Albion Baptist Church, Brisbane

Foreword by
REV. JOHN THOMAS

AMBASSADOR

What is Revival?
© Copyright 1995 Ambassador Productions Ltd.

All rights reserved

ISBN 1 898787 30 1

Printed and Published by
AMBASSADOR PRODUCTIONS LTD
Providence House
16 Hillview Avenue,
Belfast, BT5 6JR

FOREWORD

I can heartily recommend this book to all who are waiting and watching and working for the experience of a fresh impact of quickening power from heaven. In spite of the lamented stagnation of such religious experiences at present, this little book is by no means inopportune. We are being caught at present between two currents in the evangelical world. With a great number of earnest Christians the emphasis of the hour is laid on the expectation of our Lord's return to close the present age, and this emphasis is so pronounced that the expectation of a great religious Revival is almost ruled out. The longing for, and expectation of, our Lord's glorious manifestation has in a measure substituted itself for the old passionate longing for the descent of the spiritually quickening power of Pentecost. But it is equally true that, although with less self-assertion and demonstration, there is a great longing in the hearts of thousands of believers for the advent of another great Day of spiritual Revival rather than for the abrupt closing of the present age. My belief is that this desire is growing in intensity and in assurance, and that a great many, whose expectation has been focused on the glory of the skies, are finding it possible to return to an earnest expectation of the spiritual glory of the "upper room". Two such mighty expectations should not be allowed to cancel each other, but to work together for one glorious end.

The atmosphere of Revival which Mr. Morgan maintains in his treatise is one of experience as well as of meditation. He has felt the CATARACT rush over his life, and has made this manifest in the message of his ministry. He is one of a good number of Welsh ministers who received from the latest great Welsh Revival, either directly or indirectly, a spiritual impetus which altered the passion and purpose of their lives. The men who came under this special influence have exercised a deep influence on the religious life of the Principality, and it may be that from the sparks they have kindled another flame of spiritual power will yet flow over this land of Bible faith and spiritual music.

Mr. Morgan's book is not a detailed narrative of historical Revivals, but a careful study of the religious and spiritual elements that have been common to all the great Revivals of faith and vision and passion through the Christian centuries until now. His work is well done, with much real knowledge and thought and spiritual imagination. I join with him in desiring a new passion and preparation for a great Revival. There are many hindrances. But is there anything too great for the Lord?

JOHN THOMAS.

DEDICATED TO

MY MOTHER

and to the
Congregations of the Churches I have served:

BAPTIST CHURCH—BETHANIA
Cwmbach, Aberdare

ALBION BAPTIST CHURCH
Brisbane, Queensland, Australia

CONTENTS

		PAGE
I.	THE ROMANCE OF REVIVALS	9
II.	THE PSYCHOLOGY OF REVIVALS	19
III.	THE MYSTICISM OF REVIVALS	26
IV.	THE THEOLOGY OF REVIVALS	37
V.	THE PATHWAY TO REVIVAL	56
VI.	THE CROSS THE KEY TO REVIVAL	65
VII.	THE OPEN DOOR FOR REVIVAL	75

I

THE ROMANCE OF REVIVALS

If the origin of a Revival is hidden from view, reaching back, it may be, as a subterranean stream, to some secret, unknown source, so again the end of it is lost to view, where the river meets the sea. It brings blessings; it also brings with it many new trials. Even in its joy there is often cause for trembling.

From its deep springs, the flowing streams issue forth—some of them silent and sunny, some of them swift and irregular, overflowing their banks. We are not always sure of the spring, but when it flows, we know and feel its healing power.

When we see some public character accomplishing distinguished service before the eyes of the world, and leaping apparently from obscurity to fame in a moment, we are apt to forget that back of that brilliant success there lies some little incident that happened, perhaps long years before, but which really struck the keynote of that life, and prepared that individual for the public service which the future held in store.

God is always preparing His workers in advance; and when the hour is ripe He brings them upon the stage, and men look and wonder upon a career of startling triumph which God had been preparing for a lifetime.

God is preparing His Revivalists still, so when the opportunity comes He can fit them into their places in a moment while the world wonders where they came from.

The chariots of God are twenty thousand, and some of them, in the opinion of His Churches, are pirates. The government is still upon His shoulders and He fulfils Himself in many ways. Instincts, impulses, affinities, even prejudices at His bidding speed, and the word of the second Psalm gets a new meaning and application. Why do the critics rage, and the psychologists imagine a vain thing? The kings of the Church set themselves and the rulers take counsel together. But He that sitteth in the heavens shall laugh. The kingdom of heaven advances and expands by strange and sometimes unorthodox ways. There is every possibility, for instance, that we owe the Protestant Reformation to a hat! A certain plain, modest, old-fashioned schoolmaster, named John Trebonius, always took off his hat in the presence of his scholars. "For who knows," said he, "there may be among my pupils a great poet, or a great preacher, or a great philosopher!" And, as a matter of fact, he had in his class a chubby little boy whose name was Martin Luther—so called by his parents for having been born on the eve of St. Martin. Martin Luther's tutors were many —yet not many of them are known to fame, and John Trebonius is remembered, not for anything he said, but for something he did and his explanation of it. To the simple removal of that man's hat, I suggest, we may owe the Reformation.

A young Welsh clergyman, in reading the Litany one Sunday morning, came to the words, "By Thine agony and bloody sweat," and saw for the first time the stupendous meaning of the words. That started a Revival that changed the character of the whole of Wales which is called "The Great Revival".

It is said that on the morning Daniel Rowlands uttered that portion of the Litany, he uttered the words with such overpowering feeling and thrilling tenderness that the people could hardly bear them. They seemed to be in Gethsemane with their Lord, far in amid the darkest shades of the awful garden. A cry of agony went up from the whole congregation, and it seemed as if there and then they were filling up that which was behind of the affliction of Christ.

Rowlands had to pause, and it was some time before he could go on with the service.

Llangeitho became the centre of the great Revival. Communion Sunday became the greatest of all days. It was the great day of the feast for the whole country within a distance of thirty miles or even more; in fact people came in throngs from all points of the compass. It is said that Rowlands was up earlier than usual on Communion Sunday morning. He spent most of the time before the morning service in front of his house in the meadow, which the clear waters of the graceful Alton touch as they gently flow by. There, within sound of the meandering stream, the great man of God pondered over his message until he heard among the hills the echoes of the Psalms of Praise, as sung by large companies of the joyful pilgrims on their way to the feast. The hour was at length come. the apostle of his country would listen to the sound growing louder and louder as the numerous bands drew near, until at last the glen was flooded with gladsome music. He would then exclaim, in an ecstasy of delight, "Here they come; here they come! bringing heaven with them!" The service was generally held on such occasions in a field close by, as the sanctuary was far too small to hold the multitude who congregated together, and the flame of Revival created Calvinistic Methodism in Wales. In those glorious days William Williams of Pantycelyn was the greatest convert of this Revival, and its greatest helper. Had the Revival done nothing but this conversion it would have been enough. Wales owes him a great national debt. Williams became the singer of the Revival—author of hundreds of Welsh hymns, and two well-known English hymns—

"Guide me, O Thou great Jehovah,"
and
"O'er the gloomy hills of darkness."

The Romance of Revivals

Christianity was born in a Pentecostal season, and evangelical religion has always been characterized by seasons of refreshing from the presence of the Lord. The laws of rhythm in human life, and the principles of social and crowd psychology, show how normal and necessary are regular worship and the discipline of prayer, with a regularity of sleeping and waking. Yet this same law points to the wider rhythm of seed-time and harvest, summer and winter, and demands its own appropriate expression in seasonal, social and religious gatherings of a more imposing and impressive order. This is the psychology of Saints' days, anniversaries, and special periods for dedication or for missions and revivals. On these occasions, local and religious associations, personal memories, the spirit of expectancy, and a sensitiveness to spiritual meanings all combine with the appeal of hymns, music and the message to create that attitude of like-mindedness in which great and immeasurable things become possible.

By the Great Revival under Daniel Rowlands, a new consciousness was born in Wales. The Welsh Charity Schools by the exertions of the Rev. Griffith Jones, of Llanddowror, began to speak; people in general expressed a willingness to receive instruction, and the Church flourished.

We know not from whence Revival may come. It came to England in the eighteenth century, to a strangely and wildly disordered world. Wesley's generation saw recurrent wars with France, Spain, and Austria, and heard the mutterings of civil war in Britain. It witnessed the beginnings of the Industrial Revolution at home, and the full course of the American Revolution on the other side of the Atlantic. The crowds to whom Wesley spoke lived in towns and villages where violence, drunkenness, destitution and smuggling were rife. Education was the prerogative of the few, and illiteracy general. It was in a land and age whose common life was crude, that John Wesley's heart was strangely warmed, as he listened to one who was expounding and explaining a passage in the Epistle of Romans, and from that time he knew that his sins were forgiven—he was a changed man; and so he went as a flaming evangelist from place to place, wherever opportunity offered, preaching to thousands upon thousands. The Reformation was a return to the teaching of the New Testament. The Evangelical Revival was a return to the spirit of the New Testament and especially to the Christ of the New Testament.

As the Evangelical leaders came closer to the mind of Christ, they became better able to follow Him and to interpret Him to their generation.

"The wind bloweth where it listeth." It came to England sixty years ago from a shoe-shop in Chicago; it came in the eighteenth century from a dingy little room in Aldersgate Street, London. The American Revival, for example, came unexpectedly from Fulton Street prayer meeting for business men; the unique visitation at the Kirk of Shotts in 1630 blossomed from the communion service; and the Ulster awakening followed a three months' intercession by a number of young men.

Roman Catholics look askance at the Evangelical Revival—yet John Henry Newman was one of its products. Missions as a rule do not appeal to the members of the medical profession, yet Wilfred Grenfell, the greatest living medical missionary, is one of Moody's converts.

It came to Palestine 1,900 years ago from an upper room in which a little group of men and women were "continuing daily in prayer to God."

It came, with a "rushing mighty wind" echoing through the upper room where the one hundred and twenty waited and prayed. The tongues of fire descended, and the kindling flame sat on each of them. The Holy Ghost came. Then Peter mounted at a bound into supernatural insight and endurance and fearlessness, as if a stripling tree should attain suddenly the vigour of a majestic oak. God possessed him; he lived, yet not he—Christ lived in him. He was invincible. He was invested with boldness at which the rulers and elders and scribes marvelled. The result was the Pentecostal Revival—and something happened.

It came, when Jonathan Edwards took for

his text the words, "Your feet shall slide in due time." The Spirit of God came upon the congregation in such a powerful manner that the unconverted felt as though their feet were already sliding down to hell, and in terror cried out, "What shall we do?" and a gracious Revival followed.

It came, after Christmas Evans, the Welsh preacher, had spent three hours in a wood waiting upon God in prayer, broken with sorrow, because he felt his spiritual life very low and cold. "I was weary," he says, referring to this period, "of a cold heart in the pulpit, in secret prayer, and in the study." "Having begun," he said, "in the name of Jesus, I soon felt, as it were, the fetters loosening, and the old hardness of heart softening and, as I thought, mountains of frost and snow dissolving and melting within me. There stole over me a sweet sense of His forgiving love. As the sun was westering I went back to my appointment. On the following day I preached with such power to a vast concourse of people gathered on the hillside that a revival broke out that day and spread through the whole Principality."

It came, when John Elias, the famous Welsh preacher, after much prayer and supplication, with great brokenness of heart, more especially because of the inhabitants of a very godless district, who for years had been in the habit of holding a fair on a certain Sabbath day, in the strength of the Lord prepared for the occasion, and was able to preach with such power and unction that a mighty revival took place, and from then there was never known to be another fair held on the Sabbath.

It came, in 1904, to a remote village in Cardiganshire, which was a prelude to the great Welsh Revival—when, at a meeting of young Endeavourers, a young girl was lifted from her seat, and in spite of her natural and pronounced shyness, with trembling lips was inspired to say fervently in Welsh, "I love Jesus Christ with all my heart." It was all so unexpected, so beautiful, simple and sincere, so manifestly of the Spirit that it acted like a spark on tinder. The weeks that followed were unforgettable and, in August, 1904, the great outpouring burst forth.

The fire gained strength presently to leap forward in an irresistible flame. At a Convention, in a Methodist Chapel at Blaenanerch, the year-long prayer of young Evan Roberts, the miner-student of Loughor, received its mighty answer.

Trembling, with his arms cast over the bench in front, fearful yet humbly persistent, praying to be bent to the divine will, he made his unconditional surrender, received the Spirit and rose to his feet on fire with the love for every soul in Wales. Thus the Revival brought forth its most prominent leader, and its greatest days began. "Put away your sins! Forgive everybody! Confess Jesus! Obey the Spirit!" he cried from crowd to crowd, and thousands of commoners assumed their royal priesthood and became co-workers in the Revival. Soon, he gave up preaching and pleading, and the Revival became an indispensable nation-wide prayer and praise meeting, which in many a heart goes on and on—and will throughout the ages of eternity.

It came, because all these channels saw the utter need of their day and generation, and cried, and prayed through, and the truth holds good to-day; as soon as Zion travails, "she shall bring forth". When Zion has travailed in the past, she was able to proclaim—

"Lo, the winter is past,
  The rain is over and gone,
  The flowers appear on the earth,
  The time of the singing of the birds is come
  And the voice of the turtle is heard in the land"

(Cant. ii. 11, 12).

II

THE PSYCHOLOGY OF REVIVALS

The question often asked is—"Are Revivals in the predestinated plan of God for His Church?" Are they a wheel in the great divine machinery, or something brought in to urge the work along? Can we really say that Revivals have a place in the divine economy? As the ordained methods of the world's conversion, do they enter into the system of redemption?

In the first place we have strong reasons to believe that Revivals are God's plan for His Church, because of what they have achieved, the great harvests that have been gathered, and the gracious blessings that have come to humanity through them spiritually, morally, and secularly.

Revivals have been the divine onset throughout the ages, it is the way of the unconventional God in carrying out His methods of bringing humanity back to Himself.

Many think that Revival is some mystic emotion, or ecstasy of the mind, or some illusive vision. But Revival in its origin and true sense is the Power of God lifting humanity to the true standard of life and morality through human channels. It is the pronunciation of the mind and will of God in regard to His ideal life for the Church of Christ in the world. The general opinion is that Revivals are only a series of fortuitous happenings in the course of time, as though everything were being carried along by some blind force, while men of spiritual genius and power are trying to control that force, like some runaway horse. This leads mankind, and the Church especially, to a materialistic state of mind, and consequently life is considered as controlled by fate. Fatalism shuts God out of the moral universe, and does not recognize His sovereign will in the affairs of time.

In the hidden ledger of God there is a specific law where every Revival works accordingly, and every law runs back to the source of all things, even to the wise Lawgiver who planned, the Mind that thought, the Heart that felt—the God that purposed everything in the end to reach the goal of perfection.

We see God manifesting and working through matter, possessing everything around us, His creative power bursting forth in leaves, buds, blossoms, and fruit. Consider the blood stream coursing through the human frame; how rich it is with nutriment to nourish the cells, nerves and tissues, bringing life-virtue and cleansing throughout the whole human constitution. When the divine life flows and streams into the believer by the power of the Holy Spirit manifesting and operating on the heart, it elevates the will and purifies the moral functions of man, bringing his moral powers into subjection to the law of God.

All the worlds around us are floating in the ocean of His love. Eternity swings in all its activities on the hinges of His will. The creating, providing, redeeming, burning presence of His love causes the hosts above to fall and worship. Revival is stepping in line with the spiritual law of God—for God is an eternal revival in Himself.

It is reviving humanity, strictly speaking, to the sense of God—through the indwelling of the Holy Spirit—to reanimate the life of the believer, not the unregenerate, as they are "dead in trespasses and sins." There could be no reviving, as there was no life to revive. But whenever Christians are revived, there will always be the conversion of men. It has a two fold meaning, implying the Revival of spiritual life and vigour among the Christians, and the conversion of sinners.

It is God manifesting Himself through human life, His redeeming power bursting forth in fruits of righteousness and holiness, in the constitution of His Church.

The reproduction of spiritual life, a fresh incarnation of the gladness, the rapture, of the Gospel of the Galilean fields, of the anguished cry of Pentecost rising into a doxology of redeeming love.

Revival is a time when the Spirit of the Lord again moves on the face of the waters, and the freshness and beauty of the new creation comes forth. The divine love broods over chaos, desolation, and wreckage, again building her nest, to rear her brood for the celestial realms, where they shall one day soar and sing in the light of eternal day.

As He is an unconventional God, He is not tied down to one method of working; like nature, He has diversities of aspects attached to Revivals. Naturalists tell us that there is utility under all beauty, a practical design in all the apparent overflow and waste of the world. Utility in the song of the birds, in the perfumes of flowers, in the dyes of the sunset, in the triumphant arch of the storm.

However this may be, there is a perfect utility in the economy of redemption, and every outpouring has its practical design. Revival is not a scheme meeting a certain dreadful exigency and then of no further significance; it is the fullest revelation of divine love pouring itself out on humanity, on which the spirits of the just shall feed and feast for ever. Then the saints feel how the riches of grace go beyond their largest thought and desire. Their joy is "unspeakable and full of glory"; their peace "passeth understanding".

What is the meaning of those rapt utterances which are so frequently heard in the assemblies of the saints where liberty of utterance is allowed during a time of Revival? "Glory," "Hallelujah" and kindred expressions heard during a time of refreshing are no vague ecstatic expressions, but the voice of infinity in the soul—when language fails; they are the golden splashes of an overflowing cup, the blessedness of life overbrimming the limitations of speech.

In the first coming showers of the Welsh Revival, two old pilgrims at Aberdare, who had never forgotten the Revival of 1859-60, but had kept their Simeon-like watch—suddenly sprang to their feet at a prayer-meeting, and, with arms uplifted, shouted, "Here it comes! Here it comes! old '59!" There was no name for it, only the equation of an old and hallowed memory. It was THIS . . . .

No two Revivals are alike. The supreme Giver varies His mode of bounty with reference to differences of country and period.

Sometimes it comes like the breaking of the dawn, without any outward sign. The thing without a name—"THIS"—arrived in many guises in the past, but in all of them it was unmistakable.

Its coming was in some instances like the springtime renewing vital godliness and truth, as with the Pietists and Spencer. At other times it comes like the morning breeze trembling through the bush meadow with a whisper of heaven to His waiting channel. There are times when a Revival comes as a great hurricane; it is irresistible, like a cyclone, carrying everything before it.

Ezekiel was taken out to the valley and was asked what he saw there. "Bones, very many and very dry." He was commanded to prophesy upon these bones. He did so, and —at first, oh, how dry his throat became; at first, oh, how hollow the echoes of his voice would be, as they came back upon his ear, resounding through the valley. How pithless, how hollow, how useless—"But, lo, as I prophesied there was a noise, and a shaking, and a rattling, and a creeping." Mystery of mystery! Wonder upon wonder! There is a shaking. Bones come together—bone to his bone. "And when I beheld, lo, the sinews and the flesh came up upon them." "But there was no breath in them." Still dead— still slain—no life. Then he was told to prophesy to the wind, and he blew, and they "stood up upon their feet, an exceeding great army", vital with life.

Revival comes at times like the winds that bring bracing vigour and healing balm; that scatter the mist and woo the bud, that wake the morning and lull the evening. Where the Breath comes, prepared for by the first impulses of repentance, there follows Revival, not of one, not of individuals only, but of an entire society, of a whole nation. The same Breath comes, but never in the same way. He breathes on a Wesley, Whitefield, Edwards, Roberts—and lo, a shaking—behold a moving —a rising—but every operation displays the ability of God to reach His predestinated purpose of bringing humanity to Himself.

The Nile enriches most in its overflow. So

in the spiritual life throughout, the overflow reaches and teaches us most. We are most served by that which in some measure goes beyond us; that which awakens our wonder, gratitude and desire. The Nile of God, when it overflows its banks in any nation, is always freighted with heavenly merchandise of gold, and silver, and precious stones, and enables the heavenly argosies—built in the glory and rigged with blessing bright—to steer into port with mystic treasures which "wax not old", "eternal in the heavens".

Or, if the Revival comes as a breath, a passing breeze, it may whisper that God is near, it will freshen the stagnant flood, lift the unhealthy fog, awaken music in the stirred branches, and fill the whole landscape with animation and freshness.

"Who brought the Revival to you?" was the question once, during a fruitful season, asked of an old minister, who now rests in the deep vales of God's Avalon! "No one," he replied; "*we* got revived." It can be had wherever men and women are prepared to give themselves, with one accord, to prayer. It is "the goodwill of Him that dwelt in the bush".

III

THE MYSTICISM OF REVIVALS

Mysticism is as old as creation. It has a noble history—a divine incentiveness—and an inspiring goal.

Mysticism is the golden pipe through which the divine oil flows. It is the highway for transmission of the eternal voice and power to the inner man. By it the barriers are broken down, the heavenly light shines in, and illuminates the dark recesses of the soul, and "Lo there is Light"—Life and Liberty—pervading the personality with a mysterious influence, which is the unction of the Holy Ghost.

Rufus Jones says that "Mysticism is religion in its most acute, intense, and living stage"; Professor William James tells us "that personal religious experience has its root and centre in mystical states of consciousness"; Pfferderer states that "Mysticism is the immediate feeling of the unity of the self with God; it is nothing therefore, but the fundamental feeling of religion—the religious life at its very heart and centre". To quote the words of an Apostle, Mysticism is—"The eyes of your understanding being opened, enlightened, or insighted, that ye may know."

It is the knowledge of God in Christ through the Spirit. It is the influx of the divine Presence in the soul of the redeemed believer, and an experimental knowledge of the activities of God in the soul. Hence the chief factor of every religious revival is to bring light and life to men; not merely to move their emotion—but to create a motion Godwards in the hearts of people. Any revival that falls short of that has lost its purpose and intention in the world.

The word mysticism simply means "The cult of the Supernatural"; the realization of the believer's unification with the invisible sovereign grace of God governing the whole personality, or, according to the Lord Jesus Christ, "Abiding in the Vine", drawing all the resources of life from Him, the invisible Fount. The divine philosophy of the inner life is "I in them and Thou in Me"—"that they may be made perfectly one".

The Pauline epistles introduce us into the same thought—"Christ in you the hope of glory", "The mystery which is Christ in you", "The measure of Christ".

True mysticism is therefore, the opening of the soul Godwards—serving manwards—and radiating worldwards; every true God-given, Holy Ghost Revival does that to men and women; they open their hearts Godward.

Mystic is a German word which means "immediate experience of the divine"—first-hand experience, an intercourse with the Final

—the absolute Reality, with God in His Son! In a sense every "born again" person is a mystic, "because of the immediate experience", which comes by the faith, to every one that believes. A true mystic is not a fanatic, but one who lives in God for humanity. "For to me to live is Christ," said one of the world's greatest mystics—the surge of self into the fulness of Christ. You cannot go outside of A to Z in the realm of literature; you box the compass of language between A and Z; likewise, Christ is first and last in the mysticism of revival; it never does and cannot get outside of Him. What makes a Christian mystic is the indwelling of the divine life—the inner light of the divine Spirit shedding abroad its genial rays in the soul, and enabling it to obey the Word of the Lord.

In times of Revival this experience comes, not as a struggle or effort. It is not merely to put into practice certain maxims, or trying to attain a certain measure, but from beginning to end, and all together, it is a matter of knowing the Lord Jesus within. The mystic way of Revivals throughout the ages is the way of appreciation of the Lord Jesus Himself.

Take the charming, casual Augustine. In many fields this man's aim was to remake Western Christendom. He gave it ideals, some deplorably wrong and some divinely right. He inspired both ecclesiastic and mystic. He contributed to the upholders of the fabric of mediaeval Christianity ideas only too attractive. He gave Christians of all ages a spiritual quickening comparable with that given by St. Paul himself. He was a reader of books, a student of style, a dabbler in strange ideas. But God would not let this man alone; and the day came when Augustine took up the Book and read, "Put ye on the Lord Jesus Christ." He obeyed, and the Church of God gained the greatest teacher she knew in fourteen centuries. In his Confessions we have a graphic word-picture of his intense passion for Christ—

"Thou hast made us for Thyself, and the heart never resteth till it findeth rest in Thee."

He cries, he does not pray, "to sink in blissful dreams away, in visions of eternal day"; but to rest each moment in the bosom of the all-loving God is made to him the answer of his every need in Christ Jesus.

We recall the experience of John Wesley, in the eighteenth century in the room in Aldersgate Street on May 24th, 1738, when his "heart was strangely warmed". A new heart in John Wesley—and to put it, as our old phrase has it, conversion—meant a new appreciation of the Lord Jesus Christ in his life, and caused a mystic flame to burn throughout his life. The flame in Wesley's heart lit the whole of England. His experience was repeated a thousandfold in the hearts of the people who listened to his Evangel. Wesley's mysticism came out of his glorious experience. His work was vital because of the experience behind it. The love of Christ which had been revealed to him first as a sinner, revealed to him the possibility of being saved from his sins—not simply, be it noted, from the punishment of them, but from the power of sin in the heart. The doctrine, or mysticism, of "perfect love" transformed that century. England at the end of the eighteenth century was another country from what it was at the beginning. It could greet Wordsworth and Shelley; it could fling itself upon the long and deadly struggle with Napoleon; it could set itself to destroy the slave-trade; and it could be summoned to the great struggle for reform —political, social, and penal—which engrossed the first thirty years of the nineteenth century. It would be too much to say that Methodism was at the back of all these changes—what was at the back of them was that new conception of life generated by John Wesley's experience. The mystic experience of a warm heart was Wesley's legacy to the world. The "peculiar doctrine committed to our trust", he wrote in a letter dated August 1776 from Bristol, is the grand depositum of the Evangelical Revival.

Every Revival has brought these impulses of divine love to flame the hearts of men and women. Its philosophy is expounded in the one hundred and nineteenth Psalm, "I will run the way of Thy commandments when

Thou shalt enlarge my heart." When the heart grows big with gratitude, and vigorous with love, man is ready for any task divine wisdom appoints. Enlargement of heart always follows the definite acceptance of the law of God as the chief good. "The law of God," because of the indwelling love, becomes a song to the pilgrim on the way of life.

Brother Lawrence said, "It matters not to me what I do, or what I suffer, so long as I abide lovingly united to God's will—that is my whole *business*."

I read the records of the "Alleluia Revival, dated 1233, in sunny Italy"—"A time of merriment and gladness, of joy and exultation, of praise and rejoicing"—"and men sang songs of praise to God; gentle and simple, burghers and country folk, young men and maidens, old and young, with one accord. . . . And they sang songs of God, not man's, and all walked in the way of salvation." The Alleluia Revival gladdened the whole land with its mystic glowing experience of forgiveness.

I read of a New Year's Sunday in Wales in the year 1904. In *With Christ Among the Miners* Dr. H. Elvet Lewis says,

"A voice comes from the gallery—rough, untutored, surely unacquainted with the dialect of prayer? There is no need to ask; every sentence is a confession of an evil past and a redeeming present. It was not surprising to hear that he had been the terror of the Vale until a few days ago. To-day his Christ leads captive in triumph—His rejoicing captive! Mark one phrase of His prayer: 'O God, Thou art driving the chariot of salvation through this place to-day; don't drive too easy, Lord, drive slow; remember there are some, like myself, that can't get on if it drives too fast.' The morning service scarcely concluded at all; people left for some light refreshment, but hurried back again for the next service—overcrowded long before the usual hour. It conducted itself.

"Somewhere came the strains—to the tune of 'Sandon'—of Newman's hymn

'Lead, kindly light, amid th' encircling gloom,
Lead Thou me on'.

It was sung triumphantly—too triumphantly for the spirit of the words but not for the spirit of the place. . . . Such a meeting, such a service—how came it to be? For this was manifestly not the source of the revival, but the result of it. It was a flood, wide and shining in the light. . . . When that little meeting was over, and when I thought that there were hundreds like it, morning or afternoon, or both, all over the country, I knew the hidden sources, the unnamed tributaries, of the revival were here. Our crowded meetings, with their full-grown fervour and joy, were daily and hourly fed from these. The dew of Hermon — far-off, unseen Hermon — came down 'upon the mountains of Zion'."

The Mysticism of Revivals

This mysticism grips individuals as well as nations, and when this mystical experience grips a soul or nation there is no limitation to its range—"awakening echoes on the Veldt, among the Andes, beneath the Southern Cross, among 'Arabia's desert rangers' on the hills of Khassia, in the forests of Madagascar". It is a time when the Vision Splendid has dawned on the soul, and God has broken in and through, and there shines on the soul raptures of heavenly joy, for which an angel would gladly leave his throne. No wonder the Welsh miners—who came straight from the bowels of the earth to the Bethel of God—with their coal-black faces, and the tears streaming down, leaving white furrows on their faces—sang the mighty love-song of the Revival—the hymn of Hiraethog,

"Here is love vast as the ocean."

The song is of the marvel of divine love, flowing as vast as the oceans of tender mercies in never-ebbing floodtide; the very Prince of Life dying, dying to redeem our forfeited life. Out of the radiant depths of the wonder comes the triumphant appeal:

"Is there one that can forget Him?
Or can cease His praise to sing?"

They had caught the vision of the mystic inheritance in its present and future possibilities—which had taken away the glow from every earthly picture and from every worldly prospect—and made sorrow light and things present seem like empty bubbles and worthless dreams. It was an experience when they heard "the still small Voice" softer than the evening bells, sweeter than a mother's tones, gentler than music's tenderest notes. Perhaps it spoke as much to the senses of the soul as to the outward ear, but there is something in His Voice, wondrous beyond compare. There is something so deep, so tender, so penetrating, that it thrills the innermost being, and compels the secret door of the soul to open to the Christ that is to be Lord of all.

To some, the door to this mystic experience opens by the way of devotion—such as the Pietist and the Quakers. They walked the mystic way of devotion, that was the key of their overflowing life. To others, through suffering; it comes from the "unsunned depths" as in the life of David Brainerd the missionary; it was the sluice that opened his soul and created the passionate passion for the Indians. Others get the mystic experience through simple obedience to the truth. Take Spurgeon—"To me," he said, "obedience was the gateway through which the torrents of spiritual power flowed unceasingly to my soul."

As you study Luther's life, you find that the gateway to the mystic experience was his quest . . . the unceasing quest for reality—and when it broke on him, the rivers began to flow through his great personality—and the mystic stream brought life and light to dark Europe.

In one, it is devotion—in another, suffering; in another, obedience; in another, knowledge; but whether scholar or miner—saint or sinner—they all go to the same Person—under the same conditions—to receive the same blessing.

The contemplatives who have guided men to the higher walks of life and spiritual experience have been men who have effaced themselves in their Master's presence and have said, with the child Samuel, "Speak, Lord; for Thy servant heareth!" It is to the quiescent soul that Christ unveils Himself. Thomas Binney sang truly:—

> "O! how shall I whose native sphere
> Is dark, whose mind is dim,
> Before the Ineffable appear
> And on my naked spirit bear
> That uncreated beam?"

And yet he saw clearly that

> "The sons of ignorance and night
> May dwell with the Eternal Light,
> Through the Eternal Love!"

A farmer caught a young eagle, clipped his wings and chained him to a stake in the farmyard. The bird strained in vain against the limiting chain. He longed for the freedom of the upper air, to soar sunward and know the rapture of flight. With passing days came increasing strength; his wings grew great and strong, and when he tugged at his chain it strained and snapped. He claimed and enjoyed the freedom for which he was born.

Before a Revival, multitudes of people are like the chained eagle. Their life is passed in narrow limits because they cannot, or will not, cut their material and sensual bonds. But the mystic power of Revival fills them with strength—for He breaks every chain and enables them to soar—that

> "The sons of ignorance and night
> May dwell with the eternal Light,
>   Through the eternal Love!"

IV

THE THEOLOGY OF REVIVALS

I.

CHRISTIAN theology is the queen of sciences. In speaking of theology, we mean, not the science of religion, but divinity in the old-fashioned sense of the term—the science concerning God and divine things which is a fruit of a living faith in Him, as He has revealed Himself especially in and through His Son, Jesus Christ. We say that Christian theology is that which proceeds from a humble acknowledgement of the necessity, the certainty, the divine character of this fact of revelation, and seeks by the assistance of a higher light, so far as possible, to fathom and comprehend that which is revealed. In other words, we understand by Christian theology nothing else than what Christendom in all ages has understood by that word, inasmuch as, with whatever difference in matters of secondary import, it has continued unchangingly to build upon the foundation which has been once laid.

The centre of Christian theology is faith. "Know, then believe" is the axiom of philosophy. "Believe, then know," is the axiom of theology.

From a Peter we accordingly hear the language of theology in her childhood dress—"We have believed and know that Thou art the Holy One of God"; from a John the assurance of his fellow-believers—"Ye have an unction from the Holy One and *know* all things;" and again, "These things have I written unto you that *believe*, that ye may *know* that ye have eternal life—that ye may believe in the name of the Son of God."

The whole conflict of the Apostolic and post-Apostolic age may be termed an unceasing struggle between believing and unbelieving science.

The writer to the Hebrews, in harmony with the whole Christian revelation, said, "Through faith we *understand*," preceded by the well-known striking description of faith. "Faith is firm confidence ($\upsilon\pi\acute{o}\sigma\tau\alpha\sigma\iota\varsigma$) of that which one hopes for, an inner certainty of that which one sees not." It is true, we cannot, in connection with either of these phases, think of that which is termed Theoretical Science in the strictest sense of the word; but yet, the experiment and practical knowledge and certainty, indicated in suchlike utterances, is, and remains, none the less true knowledge, and indeed a knowledge which is born of faith. That central fact has been the predominant note of every Revival worth while—"the inner certainty" which comes by faith.

If we now extend the historic line yet further, it very soon becomes apparent that we meet with the same language as the Apostolic writers used, nay, with the same fundamental conception, in the case of the most illustrious men of the Church in earlier and later days. While, even in the heathen world, the priests were tacitly regarded as the bearers of a higher wisdom; while the secret of this wisdom was wont to be sought in the bosom of the sacred mysteries; while philosophers like Plato journeyed expressly to the East, in order, by a study of religions, to come to a deeper knowledge of God and divine things. The earliest and best fathers of the Church, on the other hand, we hear speak as those for whose vision the veil was fallen, and who now in a higher light contemplate the truth unobscured. Think of what Justin Martyr tells us in his dialogue with Trypho the Jew, concerning his own conversion to Christianity, in which—after countless errors and uncertainties—he had at length discovered nothing less than the highest philosophy; and of the striking confession of his restless seeking and blissful finding, placed on the lips of Clemens Romanus in the first of his homilies. Especially does the Alexandrine School immediately after bear the strongest testimonies in honour of faith, as the source and foundation of all true knowledge in the Christian domain.

"Unless ye believe, ye shall not understand." A Clemens Alexandrinus and an Origen proclaim countless times that no other Gnosis (knowledge in spiritual things) is possible than attained to by the way of Pistis (faith) alone. Their declaration was confirmed and reiterated by Athanasius, Gregory Nazianzen, Theodoret, Augustine, Anselm of Canterbury, Thomas Aquinas, not to speak of Chrysostom, and Luther, Wesley, and many others

The fact, emphasised by all the reformers and revivalists was, that the most perfect believing leads the way to the surest knowing; and that, according to the word of Luther, "Faith is the eye of Christians". John Calvin draws our attention to his teaching concerning the testimony of the Holy Ghost, in proof of the manner in which he represents the believer as in possession of an infallible knowledge and certainty of God and of divine things, such as is found nowhere else. Certainly it was entirely in his spirit that the Heidelberg Catechism, after the reference to the only Mediator (Question 18), asks not "Wherefore do you believe?" but "How do you believe?" And in the Netherlands Confession, Art. II, the declaration of that which we believe concerning God is succeeded by a forcible "We know". The believer *knows* according to all these witnesses, not simply *that*, but also and above all *what* he believes, i.e. in whom and on what grounds.

Every Revival is based upon the fact of faith as revealed in and through the Word of God. Every vision that has broken upon humanity since Pentecost has had its root in the eternal

The Theology of Revivals 41

Word. Revivalists have found that the Word not only contains the Word of God, but is the Word of God to humanity. They have found in the Bible a new world, the world of God; God's sovereignty, God's glory, God's incomprehensible love. Not the history of man, but the history of God! Not the virtues of men, but the virtues of Him who hath called us out of darkness into His marvellous light! Not human standpoints, but the standpoint of God.

Revival comes when men see the standpoint of God! and faith is the only medium that brings men there. It came when the Church was confronted by a new danger. Three hundred years after Paul's day, when it was safe and comfortable to live a Christian life, when the storm of persecution was over, then the spiritual tone of the Church became low. Magical rites, and a theology that appealed to the world as rational and sensible, were introduced together with lowered standards of Christian life and of Christian thought. Civilization was in danger, and the Church was enfeebled by a shallow philosophy, and by a cheap and emotional piety, by lowered standards. The faith was in danger of being lost in barbarism and the struggle for physical life.

Then it appeared that God broke in, and gave a vision and conception to a man fitted for the task of bringing the Church back to faith and God. In many fields this man's work was to remake Western Christendom. He gave it ideals—more, a vision, and he led the Church to the gates of a new world, to the threshold of the City of God. He gave to the Christians of all ages a spiritual quickening comparable with that given by St. Paul himself. It was a great day for Christendom when this man heard the voice of God in the garden when he "took up the Book and read":

"Put ye on the Lord Jesus Christ."

He obeyed, and the Church of God gained the greatest teacher she knew in fourteen centuries.

Into a decaying age, Augustine stepped forward to defend the Faith so gravely assailed. His apology was twofold—concerning at once, fact and idea. As to the matter of fact, Rome, he pleaded, was dying of her pagan vices. They had weakened her, stolen away her courage, dimmed her ancient honour, poisoned all the springs of liberty and action. Into this world he came as a flaming messenger of God, with the fact of faith in the atoning Son of God —the redeeming Word. It met the requirements of the psychological unity of the individual.

So strong was the power of the new faith, selfish men became sacrificial—weak women became strong and pure. New virtues were born unknown to Rome which were working like a healing and beneficent spirit in the heart of society. As to the matter of his ideal principle that moved Augustine to the grandest eloquence and argument, he said, in effect, "Ye were proud, O Romans, of your City.

Ye called her eternal, imperial, divine. But her history has rebuked your pride and proved her false deities. There is another city, so glorious in ideal and achievement that yours may not be named beside her. Two cities began to be with man, founded by two loves. The one by the love of self, even to the despising of God; the other by the love of God, even to the despising of self. The first is the city of the earth, whose grandest creation is Rome, which glories in self, and seeks the glory of men; but the second is the heavenly city, whose greatest glory is God, whose witness is conscience," etc. So he answered the lament of the Romans by setting over against their ideal of the state a state which incorporated an infinitely loftier ideal—stretching from creation to eternity—and faith as the condition of citizenship. His faith was daring—but fruitful. His vision was lofty—but also dynamic.

The following are the essential points in the Augustinian theology.

Man was created in the image of God—that is, with a will inclined and determined to holiness, and positively holy. The primitive holiness of man was not his own product, in the sense that he is the ultimate author of it, because he would then be entitled to the glory of it. All finite holiness, be it in man or angel, is only relatively meritorious, because it is the result of God's working in man or angel to will and to do. With this condition of holiness was coupled the possibility of originating sin. He points out that Adam's sinfulness was pure and simple self-will, self-decision.

"All men," he says, "are separated from God by sin. Hence they can be reconciled with Him only through the remission of sin, and this only through the grace of a most merciful Saviour." To gather up his theology—it was Grace from beginning to end,—the sovereign Grace of the redeeming God as revealed in the Cross of Christ. Where sin abounded in pagan Rome, Grace did much more abound.

Ten centuries saw further great changes. The barbarians were slowly brought into the human family and into the circle of the Christian religion. Out of tribal, royal and national wars arose nations of the civilized. With wandering steps, and slow, men doubtfully moved on to a larger and more reasonable, a kindlier and more human life. The Church had taught them religion as well as it knew, and its hold upon all society was immense. Its supreme organization remains the admiration of all who love the external, the envy of officials and administrators; but its life was flagging, the Church was failing to function. The response of Christendom was ambiguous. The Renaissance came; it was a rebirth indeed. The princes of the world and of the Church surrendered to the new learning, and steeped themselves in the new culture. It suggested an escape into a joyous paganism, happy in its freedom from a cramping Christian morality.

The Theology of Revivals

Men of alert mind recognized in the Church, as they knew it, the enemy of man. The Church was in danger; for there is no danger more serious for man or society than to love darkness rather than light.

Luther, the miner's son, is thrust forth on the stage of time—a monk, a mere student of Greek. Erasmus, as they used to say, "laid the egg, and Luther hatched it". In 1520 Erasmus had printed the Greek Testament, and the monk read it; and a few years later all Germany was reading it in German. The monk had translated it, with a keen sense of its value. The year 1517 was the 356th from the reformation of religion in France by the Waldenses; the 146th from the first confutation of popish errors in England by John Wickliffe, the 116th from the ministry of John Huss, who opposed the errors of popery in Bohemia; and the 36th year from the condemnation of John de Wesalia, who taught at Worms. And in 1517 Luther nailed his thesis on the never-to-be-forgotten morning of All Saints Day, containing ninety-five propositions. Luther was an enemy to the allegorical and mystical way of expounding Scripture, as precarious and dangerous, tending to fanaticism, and exposing religion to the scoffs of infidels. His memorable protestation upon the article of justification must not be omitted, if we desire the crux of his theology:

"I, Martin Luther, an unworthy preacher of the Gospel of our Lord Jesus Christ, thus profess and thus believe that this article, *That Faith alone, without works, can justify before God*, shall never be overthrown, neither by the Emperor, nor by the Turk, nor by the Tartar, nor by the Persian, nor by the Pope, with all his cardinals, bishops, sacrificers, monks, nuns, kings, princes, powers of the world, nor yet by devils in hell. This article shall stand fast, whether they will or no. This is the true Gospel. Jesus Christ redeemed us from our sins, and He only. This most firm and certain truth is the voice of Scripture, though the world and all the devils rage and roar. If Christ alone takes away our sins, we cannot do this with our works; and it is impossible to embrace Christ but by faith; it is, therefore, equally impossible to apprehend Him by works. If then faith alone must apprehend Christ before works can follow, the conclusion is irrefragable; that faith alone apprehends Him, before and without the consideration of works; and this is our justification and deliverance from sin. Then, and not till then, good works follow faith, as its necessary and inseparable fruit. This is the doctrine I teach; and this the Holy Spirit and the Church of the faithful have delivered. In this I will abide. Amen."

Thus we see clearly that Luther's theology was like that of all the Revivalists and Reformers before him. The central doctrine of the Reformation was Justification by Faith.

The soteriology of the Reformation, while

adopting with equal heartiness the objective view of the Anselmic theory, unites with it in a greater degree than did this latter, the *subjective* element of faith. One of the first characteristics of the Protestant theology that strikes the attention is the part which the principle of faith plays in all the discussions. The attention in the theology of Augustine was turned to the act of God. Now, in the Reformation, it is turned to that act of man by which the act and work of God is appropriated. This was a natural consequence of the change that was taking place in the general religious views of Christendom. The mind was not satisfied with an objective and outward salvation, however valid and reliable it might be. It desired a *consciousness* of being saved. It craved an *experience* of salvation. The Protestant mind could not rest in the Church; neither could it pretend to rest in an atonement that was unappropriated. The central fact of the theology of the Reformation was that the objective work of Christ on Calvary must become the subjective experience and rejoicing of the soul itself. If we may, in this connection, employ the simple and affecting phraseology of the dying "Young Cottager", we may say that Protestantism reposes upon "Christ there and Christ here", Christ on the mediatorial throne, and Christ in the believing heart—that it unites in a living synthesis the objective atonement with the subjective faith in it. To quote Karl Barth—

"It was just this submitting of doctrine not

to the authority of logic, but to the authority of God, that was the secret of the fathers, of *their* Reformation, and of the Churches they founded. The essential characteristic of their genius was not any special insight or type of godliness but their clear understanding of the basis of things; they knew that that basis was God and God alone. In other words, they had the courage to allow so accidental, contingent and human a thing as the Bible to become a serious witness of the revelation of God, to allow a book which is itself profane to become Holy Scriptures. And so, not otherwise, the doctrine, the message, the preaching arose."

Luther's scholastic and intellectual side appears in his theology, in his exegesis of Scripture, and in his polemic which was necessarily involved in others. Mysticism is a recognizable quality in his work. He professed gladly his indebtedness to the mystics, especially Tauler; and he owed not a little to the influence of the pious Staupitz. But the power that moved the world through his heart was faith in the Son of God. He proclaimed with no uncertain sound—

"THE JUST SHALL LIVE BY FAITH."

II.

"In the evening I went, very unwillingly, to a society in Aldersgate Street; where one was reading Luther's Preface to the Epistle to the Romans.

About a quarter before nine, while Luther was describing the change which God works in the heart through faith in Christ, I felt my heart strangely warmed. I felt I did at that moment trust in Christ, and in Christ alone, for my salvation. And an assurance was given me on the spot that He had taken away my sins, even mine, and had thus saved me from the law of sin and death"—(*Wesley's Journal*).

The experience of John Wesley when, two hundred years ago, on that momentous night at Aldersgate Street, his heart was "strangely warmed", marked, as the rationalist historian Lecky has said, "an epoch" in English history. Once again, by this divine experience, as had been the case with St. Paul, Augustine, and Luther, God raised up a man through whom He could reveal His Son and transform the generation to which he belonged. The experience represents a first-hand type of Christian faith. Broadly speaking, the origin of the Evangelical theology was born within the borders of the Church of England. Just as the Assize Sermon of John Keble in 1833 is taken as the starting point of the Oxford Movement, so the foundation of the Holy Club by Wesley at Oxford, in 1728, may be taken as the birth of the Evangelical theology—the strength of which lay largely in its appeal to the emotions.

The title generally given to the Movement shows that it was inspired by no new doctrine. The word "Evangelical" discloses the source of the inspiration of the Movement. It is to be found in the simple principles of the doctrine of Christ. It was not in the least partisan. It had to do with the spirit rather than with the letter of the Gospel, with experience rather than with dogma; with life rather than with the law; with the inner light rather than the acceptance of authority; with love rather than Church membership.

The word "Revival" also denotes that no new doctrine was being taught by the Movement. The truths on which it laid stress had been forgotten, or else accepted as a matter of fact for merely intellectual assent. They had lost their force and freshness. The movement brought them to light and life once more. It recovered and recaptured some of the power which they had possessed in apostolic days.

The Evangelical message was summed up in the words of St. John the Baptist recorded in the Fourth Gospel, "Behold, the Lamb of God which taketh away the sin of the world" (i. 29). This presupposes a degree of sinfulness; of wickedness, to put it more plainly, which prevented man from attaining that level of righteousness and that degree of holiness and happiness of heart and mind, which ought to be the lot of man as created after God's likeness. The alienation of man from God was removed by the Cross, and its removal has won for the death of Christ the title of the Atonement, the means of reconciliation, the at-one-ment between us and God. The Evangelical theology was seen at its best in the

The Theology of Revivals

Atonement, for its clear message of forgiveness through the Cross of Christ has brought pardon and peace to millions of souls.

John Wesley faced a rude and cruel world with the Cross as the central theme of his message. The slave was still in his chains; the prisoner in his filth and degradation; the worker in his poverty. There may have been faint signs of the stirring of national conscience, but they would be hard to find in the early days of the eighteenth century. The country had gone through the strain of the Reformation and the violence of the Puritan revolution. It asked for nothing better than to be left alone. It was afraid of any sign of enthusiasm. It was on the defensive in the things of the Spirit. Historians paint a very dark picture of life in England in the eighteenth century. Thomas Carlyle used to speak of it as "a bankrupt century", bankrupt not in money but in morals in religion and high ideals. But Wesley's and Whitefield's message of the Cross was the message the times needed supremely. The common people of England received the Good News with gladness and enthusiasm. It gradually changed the whole spirit of English Church life. It introduced a new style of preaching. These Evangelists brought a living message from burning hearts. It was full of salvation, and of appeal, convincing and converting. The heart of the Evangelical theology was the forgiveness of sin, and cleansing from sin.

The ethical ideal of the Revival under

Wesley was the ideal of essential Christianity. In 1743, when the name "Methodist" was rousing England to curiosity and questioning, John Wesley wrote a pamphlet entitled, *An Earnest Appeal To Men of Reason and Religion.* This pamphlet was designed as a reply to the question "What is a Methodist?" Wesley said: "We see, on every side, either men of no religion at all, or men of a lifeless, formal religion. We . . . should greatly rejoice if by any means we might convince some that there is a better religion to be attained—a religion worthy of God that gave it. And this we conceive to be no other than love; the love of God and of all mankind; the loving God with all our hearts, and soul, and strength, as having first loved us, as the fountain of all the good we have received, and of all we ever hope to enjoy; and the loving every soul which God hath made, every man on earth, as our own soul."

He added, quaintly: "This love we believe to be the medicine of life, the never-failing remedy for all the ills of a disordered world, for all the miseries and vice of men." The rediscovery of the Wesleys was that a complete love of God and man was the soul and substance of religion. It was with this "medicine of life" as revealed in the Cross of Christ, that he and his fellows set out to remedy "all the ills of a disordered world".

In England, as elsewhere, in Wesley's time many things had risen to dim the brightness

The Theology of Revivals 53

of the glory of the Cross—some from the very heart of the Church; some from intellectual collisions of the age. Suddenly, it broke into view—towering not only "o'er the wrecks of time", but over its proudest peaks as well—appeared the Cross. Men and women who had all their lives looked on the hills of home, now in winter's grey, now in summer's gold, saw clearly the "green hill far away", and their dear Lord hanging on the middle cross of three.

The other Revivals, too, strike the same note. The eighteenth century Revival in Wales first breathed Sinai's air but its return was to Calvary. Daniel Rowlands spent some years preaching "The stormy law"; Howell Harris, at first, made "the cloud his abode" and "the thunder his dwelling-place" but they all came to

"Survey the wondrous Cross
On which the Prince of Glory died."

Its light shone forth on the banks of the Llwchwr, in the autumn of 1904, proclaiming the same unchanging love, as it shone in the past, in its throbbing mysteries. All the richest gems of heaven's virtues are set in this one coronet—the Cross. It was the matchless thought of the eternal counsel of the Triune God. Here Luther had his gem of justification, and Wesley his gem of sanctification—and Evan Roberts his gem of the fulness of the Holy Spirit. Every Revival had a new focus of the Cross. It became the norm of their Gospel; the Logos of the Cross, to the Revivalists, was the key which unlocks the riddle of the universe, solves all mysteries and reconciles all things; thus the "word of the Cross" is "made unto us wisdom", as well as righteousness, sanctification and redemption.

Christian theology in the Revivals did not come into being because the human intellect loves to spin speculative cobwebs. It arose because of certain religious experiences which came to these leaders. It is just an attempt to explain those facts and those experiences. But there is no finality in the interpretative process. Out of the older theologies new ones are ever being born. To so lofty and stimulating a quest for truth does the God of Truth summon us to "survey the wondrous Cross" whose power knows no variableness, neither shadow of turning—its saving power remains all undiminished. Everything may change. Seasons may come—seasons go; snows fall and snows melt; islands disappear and sink beneath the waves; glaciers shift and move and slide out into the sea; mountains are rent asunder by the upheavals of nature, or levelled by the blasting and drills of men; stars fall from the heavens, constellations shift in their orbits; the wind blows hot, the wind blows cold— all these things; but the power of the Cross changeth not. The torrent bites with foaming teeth into hard granite, devouring the rocks with its tumble and roar, and carves new paths for its galloping feet as it leaps towards the sea—but the Cross still stands unchanged! Fashions are made, fashions are changed; friendships are formed and friendships are shattered—but the Cross still stands! Empires that mingle as freely to-day as the river with the ocean, may to-morrow be lashed by the frenzy of war and seethe with deathless hatred; treaties signed by mighty men may be cast aside as "scraps of paper". But though kingdoms totter and universes reel, and the sun grow cold in the heavens, His Cross will tower o'er the wrecks of time, and still as in days of yore retain its ancient power to draw all men. It was the Gibraltar of the Reformation—the "medicine of life" in the Evangelical Revival—"the never-failing remedy for all the ills of a disordered world." It was divine Logos in the Welsh Revival, to all the mysteries and riddles of life.

When Bernard of Clairvaux preached from the top of the hill at Vezelai, there rose from the sea of faces, we are told, at first, a murmur; then a shout of "Crosses! Crosses!"—and his Crusade was made. Now in a more practical century, there yet waits a sea of faces—waiting for no art wrought cross—but for a radiant interpretation of the message of Calvary's Cross.

"Love so amazing, so divine,
    Demands my soul, my life, my all."

V

THE PATHWAY TO REVIVAL

THERE is a familiar story in Eastern history which gives us a word picture of a great monarch seated in his tent on the eve of battle meditating on the great and decisive event of the morrow. He and his officers are busy making final dispositions and arrangements, the sentries are set, and they wait with patience for the great trial of strength which is so near. Hark! The sentry is challenging at the king's tent entrance; a moment later the covering is drawn aside, and escorted by the officers of the monarch's household, the heir to the throne enters. A few words serve to explain the cause of the interruption. A trivial one it may appear to us, but evidently to the prince it was a serious matter. "His sword was shorter than those used by his comrades, and alas! it was shorter than those of the enemy."

In those days when the conflict was a hand to hand fight, every advantage was coveted by the warrior, and he counted himself unfortunate if his armour or weapons proved inferior to those of his foemen; for it was a question of life and death to him.

"Thy weapon is too short," repeated the king. "Take a step forward then and so

The Pathway to Revival

reach thine enemy." The prince left his father's presence having learnt a new lesson, and by his valour and noble initiative more than compensated for the shortness of his sword.

The above is an apt illustration of our position as Christians when brought face to face with the great subject of Revival in the Church in these days. We see the stupendous task before us, the might of the enemy entrenched in apparently unassailable positions, the worldliness and coldness of the Church, the abounding false teachings—and the shortness of our weapon. But we forget that we have the privilege of exercising courage and personal initiativeness. We must take a step forward—and in the strength of our divine King's guidance and counsel face the foe with our swords—short though they may be. The first step in Revival must be a forward step.

Washington crossed the Delaware when it was pronounced impossible except by boats. Xerxes crossed the Hellespont with his million men, but he did it by bridge. The Israelites crossed the Red Sea; but the same orchestra that celebrated the deliverance of the one enemy sounded the strangulation of the other, for they listened to the command of the Controller of the elements. "Go forward!" was His command, and when they obeyed, the obstacles vanished; for when they are touched by faith they vanish away.

There is a beautiful tradition among the American Indians that Manitou was travelling in the invisible world, and one day he came to the barrier of brambles and sharp thorns which forbade his going on; and there was a wild beast glaring at him from the thicket; but, as he determined to go on his way, he pursued it, and those brambles were found to be only phantoms, and the beast was found to be a powerless ghost; and the impassable river that forbade him rushing to embrace the Yaratilda proved to be a phantom river. Yes, there are a great many things that look terrible across our pathway for a world-wide Revival, but when the Church will really advance upon them it will find they are only phantoms, only the apparitions and doubts and delusions of a faithless Church. Difficulties vanish when the forward step is taken. Put your feet into the bosom of the water, and the Jordon retreats. Go forward in the name of Jehovah and the phantoms flee away. Take a step forward into the ranks of the enemy and they are a conquered foe.

Doing away with technicalities and phraseology, Revival is taking a step forward into the ranks of our foe, invading the hopeless and lifeless with the power of God.

Revival! I almost catch the flash of the Christian's eye as the word is uttered, for to the saints of God it means the solution of many of their worst difficulties in the Christian life.

We must be careful to separate the Revival from its adjuncts and accessories. We must distinguish it from the false and dangerous excitements which have usurped its name. Even the wildest out-breakings of religious extravagance and fanaticism and superstition are dignified by the name Revival. And yet the term is properly used with some latitude of meaning, for words often become broadened in their signification, and they often convey the mental treasures of one period to the generations that follow; and laden with this, their precious freight, they sail safely across gulfs of time in which empires have suffered shipwreck, and the languages of common life have sunk into oblivion. How many words men have dragged downward with themselves, and made partakers more or less of their own fall. Having originally an honourable significance, they have yet, with the deterioration and degeneration of those that used them, deteriorated and degenerated too. The word "Revival" has suffered by friend and foe perhaps more than any other word of the Saxon tongue. It comes from the Latin word "revivere": "To live", "to return to consciousness", "to re-awaken", "a renewal of fervour". Strictly speaking, it means to bring to life again, to "reanimate", and has to do definitely with the Christian. It could not be said of the unregenerated, as they are "dead" in trespasses and sin. There could be no reviving with the dead. That which has never lived, could not be reanimated. Therefore it is a word that concerns the Christian; but wherever there is a reviving there will always be the conversion of sinners. It has a twofold meaning, implying the renewal of spirituality and vigour among the Christians, and secondly, the conversion of sinners. It is the reproduction of spiritual life, a fresh incarnation of Pentecostal life with its joy and anguish, rising into a doxology of redeeming love.

Revival is a time when the winds of God move on the face of the waters, and create the freshness and beauty which is the feature of the new creature, and the multitudes lying in the valley find that it becomes to them a "Valley of Decision".

Genuine Revivals are the fruit of the Holy Spirit—the Spirit poured forth from on high, which is life-giving—light imparting—the divine energy—which is the living, breathing, glowing presence of the third person of the blessed Trinity.

Revival—to return to our first figure—is a stepping forward into the Golgotha of bones; and there is nothing more removed from life than dry bones—breathless skeletons. Preaching to these bones is dull work; yet we are commanded to preach; yea, we are charged with a mission to dry bones. "Hear, ye dry bones, the word of the Lord." Hopeless task, apart from the promise, "Behold, I will cause Breath to enter into you and ye shall live." We need to turn to the Breath, and say, "Breathe on these dead who rigidly hold to the formalities of their religion." What the world needs, all the world over, is not to be harangued, however eloquently, about the old accepted religion; but to be permeated and charmed and taken captive by a warmer and more potent Breath of God than they have ever felt before. The "Winds of God" create and kindle new springtime in the soul.

The quaint old Thomas Adams says: "No means on earth can soften the heart; whether you anoint it with the supple balms of entreaties, or the thunders of menaces, or beat it with hammer of mortal blows; behold God showers His rain from heaven, and it is suddenly softened. One sermon may prick a heart, one drop of a Saviour's blood distilled on it by the Spirit, in the preaching of the Word, melts it like wax.

His ways are past finding out in Revivals. We have diversities of aspects attached to Revivals. Some would have us believe that God is confined to special periods before He can give an outpouring of the Holy Ghost. The question often asked is—"Are Revivals in the predestinated plan of God for His Church? Are they part of His great machinery, or something brought in to urge the work along?" Some say that He has only special seasons whereby the Spirit moves.

In the first place we have several reasons to believe that Revivals are God's plan for the Church because of what God has wrought prominently through Revivals; the great harvests that have been gathered;

the mighty transformations witnessed; and the gracious blessings bestowed upon mankind. It has been the divine onset through the ages. The bare supposition of partiality in God must be revolting to everyone's reason. There could be no justice in the universe if the supreme Lawgiver were partial, and He only gave Revivals to certain periods. The idea is self-contradictory and absurd. For a Being who is infinite or universal to be partial brings Him down to the level of the human. There can be no more partiality in God than there can be in light and heat. Revivals can be had to-day as well as in the other centuries if we are prepared to step forward. True, the poet of Avon has said—

> "There is a tide in the affairs of men
> Which, taken at the flood, leads on to fortune,
> Omitted, all the voyage of their life
> Is found in shallows and in miseries."

But God always has His flood. We are prone to remain in the shallows and omit the divine flood. The tidal wave from God-side is always lapping the human life, ready like some mountain cataract flooding the dry bed of the river after a storm.

"Oh that thou hadst hearkened to My commandments! then had thy peace been as a river, and thy righteousness as the waves of the sea" (Isa. xlviii. 18).

"I will open rivers on the bare heights, and

fountains in the midst of the valleys; I will make the wilderness a pool of water, and the dry lands springs of water". (Isa. xli. 18).

Once again, if we meet the requirements, the fountains will again flow "on the bare heights". It is the "hearkening" on our side —it is the "giving" on the divine side. But every time it is a stepping forward to the battle ground. The beginning, the starting point, the white line of Revival, runs through the battle field in every period; for we must remember there are only two forces at grips—the forces of God and the forces of evil; the forces of love and the forces of hate; of holiness and sin; of heat and cold; the forces of life and of death. That is the battle, and the principles of Revival are embedded in this, and the call of Revival is that there shall be a dominance of life over death.

What is Revival but a revelation of the dominance of good over evil?

What is Revival but the burning of fire and heat over the slipping in of coldness?

What is Revival but the manifestation of life instead of death?

What is Revival but the radiation of health rather than the paralysing of disease?

It is the principle of recklessness against these forces, and the manifestations of life and victory. It is spiritual aggressiveness, to use a military term. It is God moving the individual and assemblies and nations into the place of battle at the strategic moment when they can afford to be reckless against sin, against coldness, and against all those things that have disease and death. But it is recklessness through the power of the Holy Spirit, not human recklessness, for human recklessness will bring a tragedy. But recklessness under the sole control of God's Word in one's life, the finality and authority of the Word, in face of all opposition and unbelief, is the conquering weapon of Revival.

The call of the director of the Field, today, is Advance—Be Aggressive—Step Forward!

> "The times are great,
> What times are little? To the sentinel
> The hour is regal when He steps on guard."

Step on guard! The times are great—the hour is regal. We of this age are not here by accident, but we are born for the times.

Wellington, when in Paris, put a single soldier to keep the approach to a bridge, but the soldier knew he had the whole might of the whole British Army behind him. And when you step out—you too have the whole might of the eternal God behind you.

Men! Women! Step on Guard—against sin, coldness, indifference, and reach for thine enemy and—

> "Unlock the zone,
> And make God's pathway round
> the world complete."

VI

THE CROSS THE KEY TO REVIVAL

Before a train can move there must be a driving force. Before a voice can be absorbed by the microphone, and carried to the controls, and flung out into space, there must be a driving force. Before the wheels of a motor-car could turn down the highway, there must, of necessity, be some force behind it that puts the "go" into it. Before the great aeroplane can soar high overhead, something has to put the "go" or "umph" into it. There must be something placed therein that impels it to go. Without the driving force the 'plane would remain immobile. Something within must give those pistons driving and firing force.

When one pushes a very heavy car, or exerts to the utmost in performing a heavy task, he puts the "umph" into it that makes it go. So there must be a motivating force behind every Revival—and the motivating force is the Cross of the Lord Jesus Christ. It is the greatest theme in the universe, for it proclaims the greatest work ever performed by the greatest Person, and it secures the greatest possible ends. All the richest gems of heaven's virtues are set in this one jewel—

the Cross. It was the matchless thought of the eternal counsel of the Triune God. As the Pleiades are said to be the hub of the universe, so is the Cross the hub of the sublimest mystery of divine revelation. It belongs to the eternal realities of the heavenly world.

The Cross is the pivot upon which the world's history has ever turned. All prior things pointed back to it, and even the future rests upon it. Remove the Cross from the Bible and we have a casket without a treasure, a body without the spirit, a tree without a root, a house without a foundation, a sky without a sun, and a gospel without a message. The sublimity of it fired every power, and commanded all the resources of the greatest intellects of every age. One quaint writer has said—

"It fired the fierce eloquence of Tertullian in the early Church, and gushed in honied periods from the lips of Chrysostom; it enlisted the life-long zeal of Athanasius to keep it pure; the sublimity of it fired every power, and commanded all the resources of the mighty soul of Augustine; the learning of Jerome, and the energy of Ambrose, were committed to its defence; it was the text for the subtle eye and analytic thought of Aquinas"; it was the pillar of Luther's soul, for it held him fast and secure to the Rock of Ages when lashed by the mad waves of error; it was the systematic symmetry of Calvin's logic; it inspired the beautiful humility of

Fenelon; it fostered the zeal of the Wesley's, and flowed like molten metal into the rigid forms of Edwards; it kindled the song and rapture of the Welsh Revival. All the great Revivals have been born from its influence and power. It has been the Gibraltar of every Revival. It was—it is the greatest and most majestic fact God has ever given to mankind.

It is true that the glory of God's handiwork is seen in the Creation, but the splendour of His heartwork is unveiled at the Cross. Creation is only a spark from the anvil, but salvation is God going to the utmost. The glory of God's handiwork shows forth the excellence of his artistic skill; the glory of His law proclaims the excellence of His righteousness; the glory of His holiness unfolds the excellence of His nature; the glory of God's eternal purpose unveils the love of His infinite heart towards humanity. Everything He possesses, every constituent attribute and perfection, are called into activity in the great plan of redemption. The finest faculties of the grandest intellect can never fathom the depths of the Cross; it is the overwhelming blaze of eternal explanation; of love and conquering grace, "the divine event to which the whole creation moves." It is the divine "umph" in which myriads in every Revival have found their all; it has been a power lifting their hearts above selfish ambitions of the natural life, to a life of holiness and victory.

From many climes and from all ages come witnesses bearing the testimony of the magnetic power of the Cross; they have been drawn from different strata of humanity, for the Cross has attracted the rich and the poor, the learned and the ignorant, the popular leader and the obscure toiler, the man with the sceptre and the man with the scythe, the heathen and the civilized, the bound and the free. It is the key of the next Revival.

Among the ancient inscriptions and paintings on the tombs of the kings of Egypt are seen everywhere the symbol of the key of life. Strangely enough it is the form of a Cross. The Cross is the deeply significant symbol of the Christian faith, and yet religious significance attaches to it not merely within the bounds of Christianity. It plays an important part as a religious symbol even in the history of the pre-Christian and extra-Christian religions. We meet it under various modifications, alike in its external forms and character as also of import, among the extra-Christian nations of antiquity as of the present day, as of the Old as of the New World. Rude and barbarous people of the torrid as well as the temperate zones, and representatives of almost every stage of heathen civilization—Greeks and Romans, dwellers by the Nile, as by the Ganges, Godavery, and Indus, Aborigines and the Islanders of the South Sea—have placed this mysterious symbol upon their monuments. In later years the Swastika Cross was used,.

first among the Buddhists of India, not as an object of adoration, but a favourite symbol of a religious sect. As Buddhist influences extended, the presence of the Swastika became one of their great symbols; to a great extent it was symbolical of their atheistic and, as is alleged, also immoral libertine principle, leading to the indulgence of every sensuous excess, also it became a symbol of a cosmical or worldly bias in the worst sense of the word—of a radical secularism. It was an attempt to disguise and convert the symbol of the Cross to something else. It became the symbol of man deified. To-day we face the same situation as the early Christians; it is either the Cross or the Swastika; Christ or man; either a Revival or recession; it all depends which key we take. Protestant countries to-day have been forced at the point of the bayonet to live under the shadow of the Swastika. Nothing but a return to the Cross of Christ can save civilization to-day from the crash of civilization. Dictatorship is marching forth with its Swastika to conquer the world. The race is on! The nations are goose-stepping to destruction—marking time to the tune of distant cannon thunder while the blood-curdling shrieks of wounded and dying rise and fall into darkened eternity!

The Church is facing a momentous crisis. There must be either a Revival or complete recession—front page glory and service, or back page obituary; a Pentecostal power or a rusty bed in a corroding funkyard. Never has a generation participated in a more intensive, colourful, and breath-taking period of events. The signs of the present day intimate without a shadow of contradiction that we are on the verge of a cataclysmal upheaval. What is the key to the situation? From the divine side it is the Cross. The answer to the riddle of the universe is God, and the answer to the riddle of God is Jesus Christ, and the answer to the riddle of Christ is the Cross. To understand the Cross is to understand Christ; to understand Christ is to understand God; to understand God is to understand the universe. The Cross then is the key to the present-day solution; for it is the key to the door of the Upper Room, and Pentecost.

The problem of the world is sin, self and Satan. The Bible does not contain many definitions. It does define sin. Sin is lawlessness; a disregard of the divine authority, and a violation of the divine order of human life, injustice and oppression of tyrannical governments, the furious violence of nations in revolt—all these are transgressions of the law of God. Lawlessness is sin; the thought of foolishness is sin; to come short of the divine glory is sin; to fail to love God with all the heart, soul, mind, strength is sin; to fail to hate sin is sin; to be destitute of any of the fruits of righteousness is sin; to him that knoweth to do good and doeth it not, to him it is sin. This is but part of the list, from the divine and unerring standard, which shows what sin is. The divine verdict is "ALL have sinned" and there is no Revival until sin has been dealt with and pardoned in the individual life. As long as we cling to our sins, God is morally powerless to remit them. What does the Word say? "Let the wicked forsake his way, and the unrighteous man his thoughts." "Repent ye and turn again." All such exhortations are followed by precious promises of the divine forgiveness; and it is definitely stated that God cannot forgive except on the condition of repentance. But as soon as we have sincerely repented, just as soon as we have honestly and heartily confessed our sins, God "is faithful and righteous to forgive us our sins." The problem of sin is settled for the sinner in the Cross of Christ.

Unconfessed sin in the believer is the biggest dam to hinder a Revival. It shuts out the blessing and keeps back the blessing from others. It chokes the development of the inner life of the individual and Church. Many a church has dammed the cataracts of Revival because of unconfessed sin. Before the Church really can have a Revival to meet the needs of the modern world, she must repent, confess her neglect of the Cross in her life and preaching. For it is the *subject* matter of preaching, with the *very essence* of that which was to be preached. This "Logos of the Cross" is conceived by Paul to be the key and centrality of God's divine plan of the ages; it solves all mysteries and reconciles all things. How far has the professing Church wandered from the "place called Calvary"?—God only knows! but we see the results to-day on every hand. It is the root cause of modernism, which leads the world to a moral suicide, and out of the turmoil, out of the catastrophe of unbelief, comes anarchy, convulsions, political upheavals, and the great revolutionary spirit of the age that is sweeping the world with its vicious "isms". Marxism, Nazi-ism, Communism, ungodly Fascism and Anti-Christ "isms" are operating throughout the world in the present day. When the theology of the present day tears from its curriculums the Atonement and the Cross, and the necessity of the new birth, and the Holy Spirit, and the crowning event of Redemption, the Second Coming—what can we expect but chaos? The lack of the vision of the Cross among God's people instigates a subtle undercurrent of demoniac forces and influences which naturally robs the Church of her subsequent victory in the winning of souls to Christ. It is estimated that 56,500,000 souls go yearly to a Christless grave. With each tick of the clock the grim hand of death reaches out to claim its victims. STILL there is a LACK OF VISION. Not only is this absence of vision instrumental in the entanglement of the unsaved in the dragnet of eternal woe, but it is a DEADLY POISON to the Christian man and woman—for we perish without the vision.

Listen to the clarion call! Come one, come all! Catch the Vision! Ages have come and gone since the great act on Calvary; kingdoms have grown to mighty power and faded into obscurity; kings have risen and dynasties have passed into eternity; times and customs have changed—and yet men's hearts have remained the same—sin remains the same—and the power of the Cross remains the same.

The eyes of the saints of all ages have been riveted upon the Cross; and through its all-powerful rays shining athwart the western horizon, they can see the happy home where ends the road on which travel the followers of the Man of Calvary. Soon the tramp of dictators will be hushed; the splendid inventions of ages, the glittering palaces of wealth together with all other monuments of the greatness of men, will crumble into heaps of ruin—but the Cross will remain unchanged!

God wants those who have caught the vision of the "wondrous Cross", who will stand in the gap, who will cry aloud and spare not, those who are willing to be a flaming torch for the burning cataracts of Revival to flow through them, to be in His hand afire with a vision of the greatest thing in the universe. THE CROSS! Shall the Prince of Glory lead you to "the green hill" without the city wall? Revival depends on the measure of your surrender to that Cross! for it is God's message in this age to a distracted world, and a defeated Church. Calvary is the one place in the universe of God *where Satan will admit defeat*. He will meet you anywhere else, and you crumple up before him. The Cross is the one place where the believer can be strong and victorious. "They overcame him through the blood of the (Cross) Lamb, and the word of their testimony."

VII

THE OPEN DOOR FOR REVIVAL

If the Cross is the key to Revival, Prayer is the door which we are enabled to open to let the flood tides of Revival pour through. Knowing the pathway, having the key, we should be able to swing ajar the door of prayer for Pentecost to sweep the world once more. The disciples were behind closed doors for ten days; perhaps they did not use the key, which was in their possession, to open the floodgates of heavenly power.

Prayer is more than supplication; prayer is the exposure of the whole inner life to God. It is more than intercession, it is realization—more than speech, it is aspiration; it is a thirst for God. Madam Guyon teaches that prayer is never matured until speaking dies and the Spirit faces the Spirit in mystic silence of the secret place. It is more than the presentation of our needs and wishes; it is the inbreathing of the divine life.

There are many features of the Prayer life which we cannot touch now. But one, such as co-operation with God; working along with God's eternal purpose, by prayer we lift ourselves into co-operation with the methods of God—not to change God's purposes, but to accomplish them; not to compel God to give, but to enable us to receive. The might of prayer does not influence God, but men, and lifts us into new atmospheres. It does not make the light, but simply takes down the shutters and lets it in. Prayer, as St. Augustine says, "brightens the heart and prepares us for the acceptance of the gifts of heaven." Prayer strengthens the faith from which it springs; it is as St. Paul calls it, the stretching out of the neck, the standing on tip-toe in earnest expectation. "Prayer," wrote one of the saints of God in his most private diary, "is want felt, help desired, faith to obtain that help." "Prayer," says another, "is helplessness casting itself upon power; it is misery seeking peace; it is unholiness embracing purity; it is hatred longing for love; prayer is corruption panting for immortality; it is the dove returning home; it is the eagle soaring heavenward; it is the prisoner pleading for relief; it is the mariner steering for the haven amid the dangerous storm."

> "Prayer is the soul's sincere desire,
>   Utter'd or unexpress'd,
> The motion of a hidden fire
>   That trembles in the breast;
> Prayer is the Christian's vital breath,
>   The Christian's native air;
> His watchword at the gates of death,
>   He enters heaven with prayer."

"What God requires and looks for," says Bishop Hall, "is neither the arithmetic of our prayers, how many they may be; nor the rhetoric of our prayers, how eloquent they may be; nor the geometry of our prayers, how long they may be; nor the music of our prayers, how sweet the voice may be; nor the logic of our prayers; nor the method; nor even the orthodoxy of our prayers; but the one thing that avails is fervency and sincerity."

Sometimes our prayers may become mere superstitious and mechanical functions, and they avail nothing in the plan of God. They may be just an idle piece of ecclesiasticism and only deaden us into spiritual torpor, or inflate us with Pharisaic pride.

There is the formal way when prayer is a mere form of words, with little or no heart; or when it is simply due to the force of habit which has lost its real power and motive.

Then there is the hurried way—hastening through it as a disagreeable and irksome duty—a duty indeed, but not a delight, and to be dismissed as quickly as may be.

Again we have the selfish way—when the real motive is to consume the coveted blessing upon ourselves—in some way to promote our own selfish advantage or pleasure.

There is the impulsive way—praying as the feeling prompts, when we feel so inclined—without any definite plan of prayer in our lives, or devout habit.

Often it is the faithless way—praying as if God never meant what He has promised.

On the contrary, there is the thoughtful way—seeking to meditate upon God's word, and seeking an intelligent understanding both of the nature of prayer and the good we seek.

The earnest way—with the attention of the mind and the desire of the heart absorbed in asking, with a determination to persevere.

The trustful way—coming in the spirit of a child; first believing that God's promises justify prayer and then that we are coming to a Father both able and willing, which leads us to the consistent way—that is, living as we pray, and so walking with God as to be in the way of blessing, and by fellowship with Him be channels for His presence to flow through us.

If prayer is the imperial power of Revival, why is it that the Church has neglected it so much? In part, it is worldliness—the worldliness of its members, who are preoccupied with the things which can be seen, and leave out of the mind, out of consideration, the things that are not seen. Prayer meetings in some Churches are too old-fashioned and out of date; thereby the imperial power and authority of the Church is cast aside. Partly it is that we are so busy; partly it is that spiritual indolence and dullness; but a prayerless Church is a powerless Church. We cannot live without our native air. Neglect prayer and you dam back heaven's supply, shut out God's light, cut off the communication of His power, the vitality of His life, the vim of

His grace, the comfort of His truth, and the cheer of His presence.

Prayer is the obstacle-remover; a prayer of faith is a mountain-remover, and a sin-destroyer. Bunyan's Christian found that the weapon of "all-prayer" was sufficient to wound and defeat the adversary who would stop him in his progress as a pilgrim. We are told that the "effectual prayer of a righteous man availeth much" (Jas. v. 16). "One shall chase a thousand, and two put ten thousand to flight." Prayer is not a cry of despair; it is a calm strong set of a human soul towards God, with the direct purpose of setting in motion great currents of divine blessings towards men. We are called into holy partnership with God through prayer and we find it does not fail. But how to wield this power triumphantly is the real difficulty for us all. "The Spirit helpeth our infirmities, for we know not what we should pray for as we ought"—neither the matter nor the manner of our prayer—"but the Spirit maketh intercession for us with groanings which cannot be uttered." Under the influence of the Holy Spirit we learn the laws of prayer. If we perfectly understood these laws, and obeyed them, our prayers would infallibly be answered. Nature is surely not more orderly than Grace. We often ask Nature to help us. She tells us to understand her laws and obey them, and we find that our appeal is not in vain. God works everywhere by law. It is by law that gold comes into existence; it is by law that gold is drawn out of the earth; it is by law it is purified; it is by law it is put into circulation as a medium of currency; all that happens by law, but it does not happen without human co-operation. The universe is a universe of law; but it postulates our co-operation if we are to receive its benefit. The world is a universe of law, but I shall get nothing of the good things out of it unless I show an active initiative; unless I take trouble and pains; unless by diligence and fruitful correspondence with the law of the world I shall not obtain those things within my grasp. There are multitudes of things in Nature which are laid there in store for me, but which will not come to be mine unless I energetically work for them, unless I energetically correspond with the method of Nature. Exactly, as truly, are there stores of blessings which God intends for you, but which He will not give to you unless you energetically correspond with His Law, with His method, by prayer. Prayer is as fruitful a correspondence with the method of God as work—as fruitful and as necessary. Some things you can obtain by work without prayer; some things you can obtain by prayer without other work; some things by the co-operation of working and praying; but no things at all without your co-operation. There is a definite submission in prayer to the divine method. Prayer is submission. Passive inaction in what is called trust is not prayer. Some people speak of

The Open Door for Revival

trust when it is only passivity. Submission is always active, and submission always involves the will; it does not dismiss the will. Unquestioning acquiescence in things as we find them is not submission, and it is not prayer. Submission means getting into line with the divine mind. That may mean conflict. It will almost invariably mean action. It will bring in volition. Prayer, from whatever standpoint you regard it, is always positive, it is never passive. Submission is not merely the suppression of desire, but the bringing of desire into line with the divine will, and if needs be changing the desire. It is coming positively into line with God's will and God's desire. That is one of the features in the law of prayer, which is most important in our prayer for Revival.

A coloured preacher once told an audience how he escaped from slavery. He said, "When I was escaping from slavery, and found myself out on the ocean, I prayed to God to help me, and He did help me. I found some boards, and got on them. Well, what did I do then? Did I stop praying, and think because I had got a few boards I could get along and didn't need the Lord's help any more? No, I took a stick for a paddle, and went to paddling and praying; and by paddling and praying I got through." There is a sound philosophy in the old preacher's talk. "Faith without works is dead." Shall we take heed to paddling and praying for Revival?

God is in great straits to-day for men and women who will throw themselves into the "gaps" and the broken-down Church bulwarks. God has called His children unto this submission of intercession—never to hold their peace day nor night; to take no rest; and give Him no rest (Isa. lxii. 6, 7). True prayer and true intercession means taking God's promises into His presence and requiring the fulfilment of them at His hand; presenting His own word to Him and seeking a fulfilment of the promises.

In the prayer life the Word of God is our method or our tool-basket. Just watch a carpenter at work. He has his favourite hammer or screw-driver. So it is with the child of God who is *constantly* visiting the Throne of Grace. For example, see the glorious promise in Matthew xviii. 19 which is our sheet anchor; 1 John v. 14, 15 is our confidence when we know that we are praying according to the will of God; 1 John v. 16 is our assurance when we are pleading for an unsaved soul; couple that promise with 2 Peter iii. 9, 1 Timothy ii. 4. Come with me to Isaiah, xlv. 11, where we have one of the most wonderful words in Scripture, "Command ye Me", as well as "Ask Me". He promises to do the "impossible" if we will only call upon Him (Jer. xxxiii.3).

To return to our main thought, the solution of every spiritual problem is to be found in the working of the divine energy. We long for

Revival, and pray with intensity and with desire that it may be released in our midst, yet there seems often to be an unaccountable delay that perplexes and discourages. Are we fulfilling the conditions? God is ready to bless if we accept His method; but we fail to provide the channels along which alone can flow His supplies. He demands a closer adherence to His appointed methods, so that, having submitted to the methods, we may learn the secret of *taking hold of the power of God* and directing it against the strategic advances of the enemy, and the active entering into God's plan.

Then we have the concentrative side of prayer. There is a danger in thinking that long prayers are powerful. God wants our prayers to be definite; we are to ask what we want instead of wandering round the globe. The Bible says, "If two shall agree on anything it shall be done". If we would concentrate more, greater things would be accomplished. How very difficult it is to be definite in prayer! There is certainly a place for general and comprehensive praying, but there is a particular need for specific, concentrated, and executive prayer. Many of the Lord's children think that when a thing has been mentioned before Him that is enough and it can be left; but the whole weight of the record of praying in the Scriptures is against this and shows us that concentration and persistence is more the rule than the exception. Too often we smother the specific with much that is general because we think that if we do not pray about a lot of things we have not really prayed. We would suggest one or two things which we are sure are vital and essential matters in relation to praying with an "issue":

(1) The heart and mind should be adjusted to definiteness of attitude and purpose beforehand. There should be no mere casualness in coming to prayer.
(2) A definite registration on the matter ought to be aimed at, and in this sense there must be a "watching thereunto". Sometimes it is only after several have prayed about a matter that the prayer is given through one which registers the verdict.
(3) Do not forget that "all prayer" in Ephesians vi is definitely related to spiritual forces and these must be taken into account in the matter of persistence. Remember Daniel!

On the coast of England some years ago a certain village of about seven thousand people of whom most were fishermen, had a very lean time. The pastor of the community called the people to prayer, and said, "We will devote an evening to prayer; we will pray the Lord to let us catch fish". Being an earnest Christian man who knew something about prayer, he spoke a few words on prayer and how God answers prayer. He told them that the whole company must centre on one thing—that God would send fish, and that they might be able through the power and wisdom of God to catch fish. One after another offered prayer. Some people were not used to concentrating on one thing, and so they began to pray about everything. He would say to them while they were praying, "Stick to your text". It would embarrass some of them, but they were, though rude, honest and earnest people, and after a little embarrassment they would begin again and pray for the Lord to send fish. Again the pastor had to keep them to the subject. One man prayed, "O Lord, pour out Thy Spirit", and then the pastor said, "Brother, stick to the fish". Finally, one woman in the congregation began to pray, and God gave her such a spirit of prayer that "amens" were heard all over the house, and the whole company was softened. She seemed to voice the need, and to utter the real prayer of every heart there. The pastor felt that they had really prayed until they believed God. So without protracting the meeting, he dismissed it. The next morning the men hung around about the store and at the corners as they were accustomed to do, not seeming to have the heart to go out for fish, for they had gone out morning after morning and had not caught anything. One man, the sceptic and unbeliever of the village, thought that all that prayer was a useless kind of a thing. So he determined to go out, and show them that God would not answer prayer. He was the only man that started out that morning to fish. He pushed his boat out into the water, and, having everything ready, he threw over the line. At once he felt a tug at the line that nearly dragged him overboard. He pulled the line up and landed a magnificent codfish. Then he put his line in again and caught fish as fast as he could. It was not long until every boat was out. They caught fish that day, and every day that season. God answered prayer wonderfully, and the fishermen had all their need supplied. There was praise and thanksgiving given to God in that village. May God teach us to be definite in our prayers.

Spurgeon, as we know, was a great preacher, but he had very long-drawn-out prayers. He had a gardener who was not a preacher but could pray. The gardener went up to Mr. Spurgeon one day and said, "Most noble lord, God has honoured you in a most wonderful way in giving you such talents, and such a lovely tabernacle, and also houses and lands and servants"—and he finished a long rigmarole with these words—"Lend me your pen-knife". Mr. Spurgeon said, "Why did you not ask for my knife straight off?" "I was desirous of teaching you a lesson in prayer," said the gardener; "when you go to God you generally repeat a long prayer and then ask for what you want, whereas you ought to be definite and ask God for what you desire right off." Mr. Spurgeon took the advice, and could henceforth pray as well as preach. May we take the same advice!

George Muller, the prince of praying saints, who received £1,500,000 by prayer alone, *took more time to ascertain the mind of the Spirit than he did to pray*. He knew how to receive the mind of the Spirit, e.g. by reading the Scriptures, personal communion with Christ and the Holy Spirit. So we ought to know WHAT the mind or will of God is, and concentrate and pray accordingly.

Susanna Wesley was a great woman of prayer. One night she had been praying for her great family. "At last," she says, "it came into my mind that I might do more than I do. I resolved to begin. I will take such a proportion of time as I can best spare every night to discourse with each child by itself." How Susanna Wesley kept that good resolution—to work and pray, and with what tremendous and earth-shaking results, the whole world very well knows.

Here is another illustration to bear out this truth. Dr. Adam Clark, the great commentator, was a slow worker, and he could only produce his wealth of literary treasure by long and patient toil. He therefore made it his custom to rise early every morning. A young preacher anxious to emulate the distinguished doctor, asked him one day how he managed it. "Do you pray about it?" he enquired.

"No," said the doctor, who was a great man of prayer, "*I get up.*" There are some things we have to get up and do—think of Moses! "Go!" was the command to Philip. If he had stopped to pray about it, he would have missed the Ethiopian's chariot. It would have been wicked and disastrous for Philip to have paused to pray for guidance. It would have spoiled everything.

Then there is the creative aspect of prayer. Every great Revival has been preceded by prayer, from Bible days to modern times. The poet knew what he was talking about when he wrote, "Satan trembles when he sees the weakest saint upon his knees". Satan's greatest dread is a saint of God on his knees; he knows his kingdom is being blasted. Prayer is the gunpowder that blasts the rocks in the quarry of humanity. It is great souls at prayer and linked with the divine that have brought Revivals to the world. Something happened when they prayed! Moses prayed, the Red Sea opened! Elijah prayed, the heavens were locked! The disciples prayed, the place was shaken! The Church prayed, Peter was released! Luther prayed, Europe was moved! Wesley prayed, England was saved! Hudson Taylor prayed, the China Inland Mission was born! Muller prayed, thousand of mouths were filled! Charles Simeon prayed, minds were enlightened! Henry Martyn prayed, and light dawned on India! John Welch prayed, Scotland knew the answer! Dr. Judson prayed, and he impressed an empire for Christ, until the stubborn granite of Burma was shattered!

Something happened, because they laughed at impossibilities and believed—

"More things are wrought by prayer
  Than this world dreams of, wherefore, let thy voice
  Rise like a fountain before me night and day.
  For what are men better than sheep and goats
  That nourish a blind life within the brain,
  If, knowing God, they lift not hands of prayer,
  Both for themselves and those who call them friends?
  For so the whole round world is every way
  Bound by gold chains about the feet of God".

Shall we meet "about the feet of God", to pray for Revival?